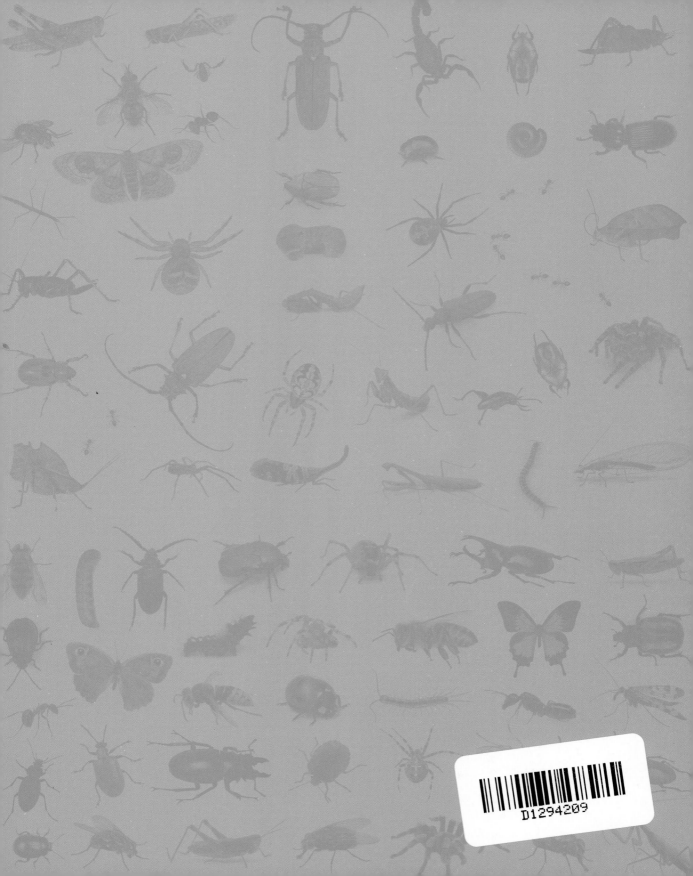

D1294209

BUGS
AND SPIDERS

Between 80–90% of the animals on Earth are insects or insect-like creatures. There are so many millions of species of insects and their cousins, spiders and scorpions, that most are not yet identified. Scientists estimate that together, all the insects on Earth weigh 300 times more than all the humans!

We're lucky that most species are beneficial to us. They are the sole food source for many types of animals. They're also vital to the process of pollination, which ensures that we have fruits and vegetables to eat and flowers to enjoy.

From breathtaking butterflies, to scary spiders, to hard-working honey bees, these amazing creatures are the most successful animals on Earth. They thrive in almost every environment on our planet.

LEARN ABOUT GRASSHOPPERS, BEETLES, AND MORE WITH FUN FACTS!

Manufactured in Malaysia in May 2020 by Tien Wah Press (PTE) Ltd.

24 23 22 21 20   5 4 3 2 1

Published by
Gibbs Smith
P.O. Box 667
Layton, Utah 84041

1.800.835.4993 orders
www.gibbs-smith.com

Gibbs Smith books are printed on either recycled, 100% post-consumer waste, FSC-certified papers or on paper produced from sustainable PEFC-certified forest/controlled wood source. Learn more at www.pefc.org.

Library of Congress Control Number: 2020932581
ISBN: 978-1-4236-5606-7

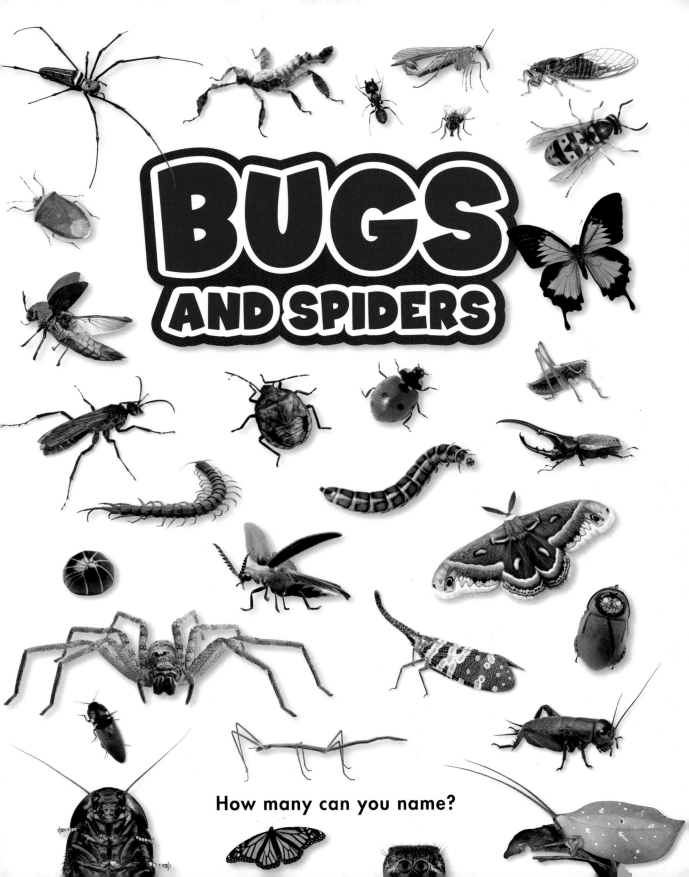

BUGS
AND SPIDERS

How many can you name?

ANATOMY AND LIFE CYCLE

Insects are small land invertebrates that have hard exoskeletons instead of backbones like humans have.

All insects have six legs and most also have wings. They were the first animals that had the ability to fly. Some people think all insects are bugs, but this isn't correct. Only some insects are true bugs. Spiders aren't insects either, although they are related to insects.

Insects are part of a larger group of arthropods, which are invertebrates that have exoskeletons, segmented bodies, and jointed appendages.

The group of arthropods includes:

- Insects, including some that are true bugs
- Arachnids, which are spiders, scorpions, mites, and ticks
- Millipedes and centipedes
- Crustaceans, including shrimp and lobsters

INSECT ANATOMY

Insects all have a hard external covering made of a material called chitin. Their bodies have three sections called the head, the thorax, and the abdomen. All insects have a pair of antennae on their heads. Their six legs are connected to the thorax. Flying insects have wings connected to the thorax. They have compound eyes, which are clusters of simple eyes.

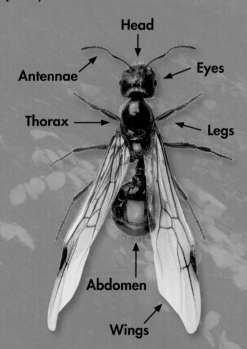

Head

Antennae

Eyes

Thorax

Legs

Abdomen

Wings

Weevil

DID YOU KNOW?
In one square mile (2.58 square kilometers) of jungle, there are more insects than the entire human population.

SPIDER ANATOMY

There are over 100,000 species of spiders and their bodies differ from insects in several important ways. They only have two main body sections called the cephalothorax, which is a combination of the head and thorax, and the abdomen. They have eight legs instead of six. Most spiders have eight eyes. They have simple eyes instead of compound eyes and unlike insects they don't have antennae or wings.

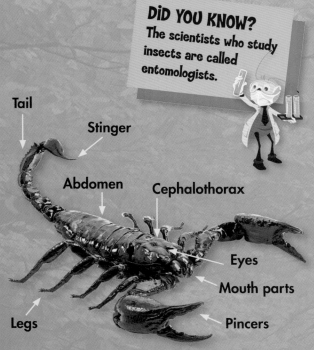

Tail

Stinger

Abdomen

Cephalothorax

Eyes

Mouth parts

Legs

Pincers

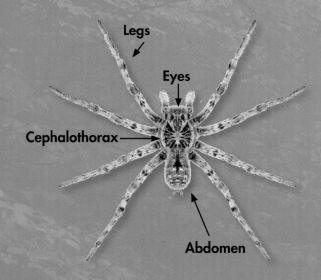

Legs

Eyes

Cephalothorax

Abdomen

SCORPION ANATOMY

There are about 2,000 species of scorpions worldwide. Like spiders, scorpions do have eight legs and don't have wings or antennae. They have a cephalothorax, an abdomen, segmented tail, and venomous stinger.

If you compare a scorpion fly, a scorpion spider, and a scorpion, you'll easily see why these animals are all related to each other.

Scorpion Fly

Scorpion Spider

Scorpion

5

THE LIFE CYCLE OF INSECTS

All insects start as eggs. Depending on the species, there are two different types of life cycle, nymph and larvae. These life-cycle changes are called metamorphosis, which comes from a Greek word meaning "change of shape" or "transformation."

NYMPH LIFE CYCLE

A cicada is an example of an insect with a nymph life cycle. When it hatches out of an egg, it's called a nymph. It looks like an adult cicada, but it's white and doesn't have wings. As it grows and gets bigger, it sheds its exoskeleton several times. This process is called molting. Eventually, it crawls out of the ground, climbs up a tree, sheds its skin for the last time, and emerges as the adult cicada with wings.

DiD YOU KNOW?
75% of insects have a larvae life cycle.

Young cicada nymph

Older cicada nymph molting

Cicada adult

SPIDER LIFE CYCLE

The female spider produces a silk egg sac with as many as a thousand tiny spider eggs. Sometimes the female carries the sac with her or sometimes she hides it under a rock, attaches it to a plant stalk, or encases it in a web. Tiny spiderlings hatch from the eggs. They look like tiny versions of the adult spiders. Spiders molt as they grow just like insects do.

Female spider carrying egg sac

Female spider carrying spiderlings

Moth eggs on stick

Moth larvae hatching from eggs

LARVAE LIFE CYCLE

With insects that are more highly developed, like moths, the egg hatches into a caterpillar or larva. The larva may feed for days or years and looks very different from the adult insect. When the larva molts for the last time it becomes a pupa. Within the cocoon, its body breaks down and reorganizes, emerging as an adult insect.

Moth pupa hidden inside cocoon

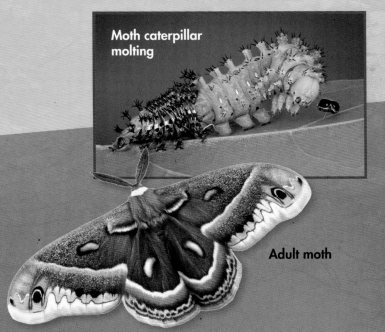

Moth caterpillar molting

DID YOU KNOW?
Insects don't have noses. They breathe through openings in their exoskeletons.

Adult moth

SOCIAL INSECTS

Some insects are solitary, which means that they live and hunt alone. Ants, termites, and some bees and wasps are social insects. Social insects work together to find food and to defend their homes. They can outcompete other insects and even larger animals for food. It's estimated that social insects make up 75% of the world's insect biomass. Some ant nests have over half a million ants, and termite nests have been found with more than three million termites!

Wasps guarding their nest

ANTS

Ants are social insects. They communicate and cooperate with each other. Not only are they social, they are eusocial, which is the highest level of animal social behavior. The word "eusocial" comes from the Greek words for "good" and "society." Their societies have overlapping generations within a colony and a division of labor into groups. The different types of workers each have their own specific jobs to make sure the work gets done for the good of the entire colony.

No other species has become as dominant as human beings around the world except for ants. It's a good thing they're not as large as we are because it's estimated that there may be as many as one million ants for every person on Earth!

ARMY ANT

Army ants are deadly. In huge numbers, 200,000 or more at a time, they leave the nest in a swarm and destroy everything in their path.

Army Ant

DID YOU KNOW?
Ants are thought to be the smartest species of insects. They each have about 250,000 brain cells.

FISH-HOOK ANT

Fish-Hook Ant

The fish-hook ant has three pairs of curved spines that are used as weapons.

Similar to how we milk cows, golden-tailed ants milk leafhopper insects for their stored nectar.

Southern Wood Ant

THE LIFE CYCLE OF AN ANT

Egg Larva Pupae Adult

Most ant colonies start when a queen who has just mated with a male ant digs a nest and seals herself in. She will rear the first brood of worker ants. This brood hatches from eggs in a week. Larvae feed on reserves in the queen's body until they become mature in about a month. Then they go out in search of food, mostly other insects and seeds, to feed the next brood of eggs. A queen ant can live for over 20 years and lay 1,000 eggs a day for many years.

DID YOU KNOW?
Native people in the Australian outback consider honey pot ants a dessert delicacy.

Honey Pot Ants

Wiki Photocredit: Greg Hume

HONEY POT ANT

Honey pot ants have found a unique way to keep food at hand. Larger workers are fed sugary nectar by other workers. These larger workers hang upside down in the nest chambers and act as a "living pantry" of food storage for the colony. When their antennae are tapped, they spit up the stored liquid.

LEAFCUTTER ANT

Using their sharp jaws, leafcutter ants harvest leaves. Then, they walk in a straight line as they carry the leaves back to their underground nests. The ants can carry pieces that are many times their size and more than ten times their weight.

DID YOU KNOW?
Army ants move their entire colonies every two to four weeks.

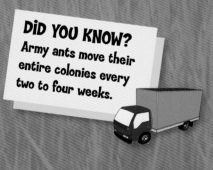

Leafcutter Ant

9

Bulldog Ant

Bullet Ant

BULLDOG ANT

Bulldog ants are very agile and can run, leap, and sting in a second.

BULLET ANT

The bullet ant delivers the most painful sting in the insect world.

Turtle Ant

Wiki Photocredit: Katja Schulz

Weaver Ants and nest

TURTLE ANT

Turtle ants have large, dish-like heads that they use to block the entrances of their hollow twig nests so intruders won't get in.

WEAVER ANT

Weaver ants are known for their amazing nest construction. They link their legs to pull and bend leaves into position. Their larvae secrete a silk used to stitch the leaves together to create a nest.

Wood Ant spraying

WOOD ANT

Wood ants are known for their incredible nest construction abilities. A colony of wood ants can create a dome-shaped nest reaching 10 feet (3 m) in diameter and 4.5 feet (1.37 m) in height! Wood ants can also spray a foul-smelling acid to ward off predators.

Carpenter Ant

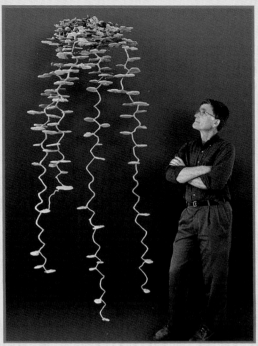

CARPENTER ANT

Carpenter ants build nests and tunnels in dead wood, trees, utility poles, and timbers of buildings. Although they do not eat the wood, carpenter ants can do considerable damage to it. The black carpenter ant is the largest ant found in the United States. This ant sometimes enters houses in search of sweet foods.

Plaster was poured into a harvester ant nest to create this amazing cast.
Wiki Photocredit: shaners becker

Fire Ants

Wiki Photocredit: TheCoz

Fire Ant

FIRE ANT

Here, thousands of fire ants are clinging together to form a floating island. They did this because a rainstorm had flooded their home area and washed out their nest. The ants will float until the waters go down, then they will get to work building a new nest.

DID YOU KNOW?
Fire ants got their name because when they sting humans it feels like being burned by fire.

BEES

Bees are flying insects that are related to wasps and ants. There are over 16,000 bee species. The smallest bees are about 1/16th of an inch (2 mm) long. The biggest bees can be up to 1.54 inches (39 mm) long. That's a big bee!

Many types of bees are social and live in colonies with anywhere from a dozen to hundreds of residents. Bee colonies can form inside natural cavities, such as hollow trees or caves. Some bees build their own homes, called hives. Bee hives are made from a tough wax that bees make with glands in their abdomen. The wax is built in the shape of hexagonal (six-sided) cavities. Many cavities join together to make a structure called a honeycomb.

Not all bees are social. Many types are solitary. Most solitary bees dig small burrows in the ground for their homes. Some live in holes, twigs, or logs. Many bees have stingers for defense. The barbed stingers can only be used once. They tear from the bee's body during use, fatally injuring the bee.

THE LIFE CYCLE OF A HONEY BEE

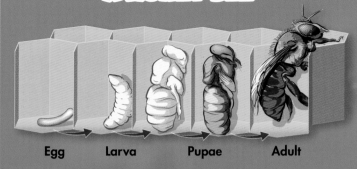

Egg   Larva   Pupae   Adult

Bees play an incredibly important role in nature. They eat a sweet liquid called nectar that is found deep inside flowers.

Bumble Bee

As they eat, their bodies get covered with a powder called pollen. The bees travel from flower to flower, collecting more pollen and dropping some off everywhere they go. This process pollinates the flowers, which means it fertilizes them and enables the flowers to make new seeds.

DID YOU KNOW?
In order to make 1 pound of honey (0.45 kg), honey bees need to visit 2 million flowers.

This honey bee's legs are covered with pollen.

A queen honey bee (marked) sits among workers on a honeycomb.

Greater Bee Fly

GREEN BEE

Green Bee

Some bees, like this member of the Euglossini species, the green bee, are brilliant in color.

GREATER BEE FLY

The greater bee fly is not a bee—it's a fly! But its color mimics a bee.

CARPENTER BEE

Carpenter Bee

Carpenter bees use their strong jaws to drill holes in wood.

Leafcutter Bee

DOMINO CUCKOO BEE

Domino Cuckoo Bee

Domino cuckoo bees lay their eggs in other bees' nests.

LEAFCUTTER BEE

A leafcutter bee carries a green leaf while flying to its nest in a small hole of a tree branch. Leafcutter bees use many leaves to make a nest.

Bees are important to humans in many ways. Their role in pollination is the most important. Bees do not just help flowers to grow; they pollinate crops, too. It is estimated that over one-third of the plants we eat have been pollinated by bees.

Farmers in parts of China are learning first-hand how important bees are. Overuse of pesticides has killed off many bee populations—and as a result, crops are no longer growing. The farmers have to hire workers to hand-pollinate the crops, using Q-tips or small brushes to transfer pollen from one flower to another. The process is expensive and time-consuming. But until bee populations rebound, it is the only way to keep crops alive.

Besides their role in pollination, bees also make many products that are useful to humans. The best-known bee product is undoubtedly honey! Yum! Certain bee species, known as honey bees, collect flower nectar in pouches inside their bodies. They carry the nectar back to the nest and dump it into honeycombs. Many bees fan the nectar with their wings to evaporate the water content. Soon the nectar gets thick and sticky and turns into honey.

Bears love honey, so many honey containers are bear-shaped.

DID YOU KNOW?
A honey's flavor depends on the flowers from which it is made. Different honeys taste completely different!

DID YOU KNOW?
Beeswax has been found in wrecked Viking ships, Egyptian tombs, and Roman ruins!

The honeycombs themselves have various uses. People use beeswax in many cosmetics, such as lip balms, hand creams, moisturizers, and some makeup. Beeswax also makes beautiful, long-burning candles. It can be used as a lubricant, a wood and leather polish, and a waterproofing agent. It is useful stuff!

Bee pollen capsules are a popular daily vitamin supplement.

BEEKEEPING

In commercial beekeeping, colonies are kept in artificial hives. The bees are free to come and go from the hives to carry out their pollination work. Beekeepers periodically harvest honey and honeycomb from the hives. This raw material is sold to manufacturers, who use it to make many products.

Some people believe that honey bee products have health benefits. Raw honey, beeswax, and other substances are prescribed as medicines to make people feel better.

Artificial bee hives

Devices make smoke to stun the bees, without hurting them, during honey extraction. This keeps the beekeepers safe from stings.

BEETLES

Over 350,000 species of beetles have been identified and there are tens of thousands that have yet to be discovered. They are the most diverse group of insects on our planet. Their bodies are tough and they have powerful jaws with mouthparts used for chewing. Adult beetles have two pairs of wings. Their outer wings are hard and are designed to protect the inner pair of wings. Many types of beetles can fly with their second pair of wings, but not all beetles can fly. Most adult beetles are brown or black, but some, like the lady beetle or ladybug, are very brightly colored.

Ladybug

DID YOU KNOW?
One ladybug can eat as many as 5,000 aphids in its lifetime.

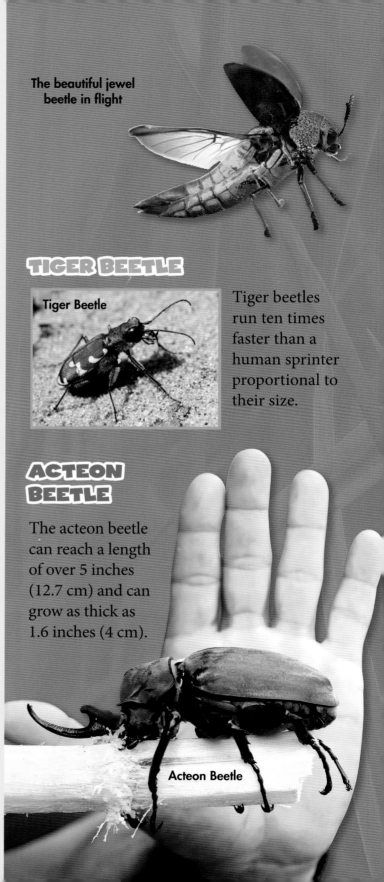

The beautiful jewel beetle in flight

TIGER BEETLE

Tiger Beetle

Tiger beetles run ten times faster than a human sprinter proportional to their size.

ACTEON BEETLE

The acteon beetle can reach a length of over 5 inches (12.7 cm) and can grow as thick as 1.6 inches (4 cm).

Acteon Beetle

THE LIFE CYCLE OF A BEETLE

Egg

Larva

Pupa

Adult Beetle

The life cycle of a beetle has four different stages: egg, larva, pupa, and adult beetle. The beetle larva looks like a worm but it has six legs and a hard head. The larva changes into a pupa with leathery skin that can't move until the adult beetle pops out.

Dung Beetles

DUNG BEETLE

Dung beetles roll poop from herbivores to their nests for their young to eat.

Frog-leg Beetles

FROG-LEG BEETLES

It's a royal rumble when metallic blue and green frog-leg beetles meet for a battle.

Trilobite Beetle

TRILOBITE BEETLE

The female trilobite beetle can retract its head into its shell like a tortoise.

Yellow Tortoise Beetle

YELLOW TORTOISE BEETLE

The yellow tortoise beetle can change colors like a chameleon.

BUGS WITH LIGHTS

Some insects are bioluminescent. This means that they can produce light that makes them glow in the dark. This feature is used for many different reasons, such as finding mates, attracting prey, scaring away predators, and signaling to other insects. It's pretty handy to be able to make your own light!

FIREFLY

Fireflies aren't flies at all. They're actually beetles. Despite their name, only some species of the more than 2,000 species of fireflies can produce light. Both the adults and larvae glow. Even their eggs glow! Scientists believe that their light is used to tell predators that they're not tasty to eat. The light show that fireflies create on warm summer nights looks magical.

Firefly

Scorpion under UV light

DID YOU KNOW?
Scorpions are not bioluminescent, but some scorpions do glow in the dark when they are exposed to ultraviolet light (also called black light).

DID YOU KNOW?
A group of fireflies can sometimes flash their lights all at the same time. Their light can be yellow, green, or orange.

GLOWING CLICK BEETLE

Glowing click beetles are nicknamed "headlight elaters." Each beetle has two light organs at the back of its head and one under its abdomen. They're sometimes mistaken for fireflies, but fireflies don't have headlights. They don't flash their lights like Fireflies do, although sometimes when they're touched their lights get brighter.

Glowing Click Beetle

Glowing Cockroach

GLOWING COCKROACH

Only one specimen of the glowing cockroach has ever been found. It was collected in the 1930s in an active volcano in Ecuador. Scientists believe that it used its lights, formed by bacteria, to ward off predators.

Wiki Photocredit: Peter Vršanský and Dušan Chorvát

Glow Worm

GLOW WORM

Glow worms are the larvae of a small type of fly. It's the only stage of their life when they glow. The adult flies can't eat, so the glow worms have to eat enough during their year of life to sustain the adult flies. Glow worms glow to attract small insects from leaf litter to the water where they live. They create snares similar to a spider's silk threads to capture their prey.

Visitors explore Waitomo Glowworm Caves in Waikato, New Zealand.

RAILROAD WORM

A lit-up railroad worm is easily seen at night.

Wiki Photocredit: Aaron Pomerantz

During the day, the railroad worm hides under logs and rocks. At night, it crawls out to look for food. If it's threatened by a predator it turns on greenish-yellow lights along the length of its body and red lights on its head. Usually, the startled predator quickly retreats.

19

BUTTERFLIES AND MOTHS

Butterflies and moths look very similar, but there are actually numerous differences between these two types of flying insects. Moths are active at night and butterflies are active during the day. While they are at rest, butterflies usually fold their wings back. Moths flatten their wings against their bodies or spread them out in a "jet plane" position. One of the major physical differences is that butterfly antennae are thin and have club-shaped tips compared to the feathery-looking or comb-looking antennae of moths. The bodies of most moths are stout and fuzzy compared to the slender and smooth bodies of butterflies. Butterflies are usually more colorful than moths. Although they go through the same egg, larva, pupa, and adult life cycle, butterflies form hard chrysalises while moths make cocoons wrapped in silk.

Butterflies are one of the most beautiful insects on earth. They go through four life stages. The female butterfly lays hundreds of eggs. Each tiny egg is placed by itself on a plant. When the egg hatches, it is a caterpillar. It sheds its skin and becomes a pupa. In its final stage, it changes into a butterfly. This life cycle takes about 30 days.

THE LIFE CYCLE OF A BUTTERFLY

Egg

Caterpillar

Molting

Pupa

Emerging Butterfly

DID YOU KNOW?
Birdwing butterflies have more angular wings than other types of butterflies. They also fly in a similar way to birds.

A butterfly drinks nectar using its long tubelike proboscis.

Both butterflies and moths have scales that cover their bodies and wings.

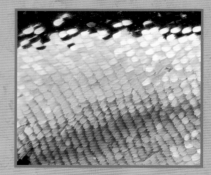

20

ULYSSES

The Ulysses butterfly has bright blue wings with black edges. This beautiful butterfly lives in the Australian tropical forest and is a type of swallowtail.

Ulysses

DID YOU KNOW?
Butterflies attach eggs with a sticky material like glue to stems and leaves.

QUEEN ALEXANDRA BIRDWING

The Queen Alexandra birdwing is the world's largest butterfly with a wingspan of almost 11 inches (28 cm).

Queen Alexandra Birdwing

Eastern Tiger Swallowtail

Peacock

PEACOCK

The peacock butterfly is easy to recognize. It has a pattern on its wings that looks like eyes in order to scare predators away.

EASTERN TIGER SWALLOWTAIL

The eastern tiger swallowtail butterfly got its name from the long tails it has on its hind wings, which resemble the tails of swallows. Its distinctive yellow and black, tiger-like stripes make it easy to recognize.

PAINTED LADY

The painted lady butterfly is also called the cosmopolitan butterfly. It's called the painted lady because of its coloring, and the cosmopolitan because it's the most widely distributed butterfly worldwide.

Adult Monarch Butterfly

Painted Lady

CHECK OUT THESE MOTHS!

Luna Moth

LUNA MOTH

The luna moth is named after the moon and has a distinctive shape with long "tails" on its hind wings. It is a pale green color with eyespots and deep purple edging on its wings.

Pellucid Hawk Moth

Hickory Horned Devil Caterpillar

PELLUCID HAWK MOTH

The transparent wings of the pellucid hawk moth make it more difficult for predators to see them. Their wings don't reflect much light so they are similar to an invisibility cloak.

HICKORY HORNED DEVIL CATERPILLAR

The hickory horned devil caterpillar is fierce-looking and can grow as big as a hot dog. It is the larva stage of the royal walnut moth.

Nine-Spotted Moth

Royal Walnut Moth

NINE-SPOTTED MOTH

With its large, white spots and distinctive yellow band, the nine-spotted moth is easy to identify.

ROYAL WALNUT MOTH

These big moths can have a wingspan over 6 inches (15 cm).

ATLAS MOTH

The world's biggest moth never eats because it does not have a mouth. It lives off the fat that it stored from food eaten during its caterpillar stage. The Atlas moth is a bird-sized insect with a wingspan of over 12 inches (30.4 cm).

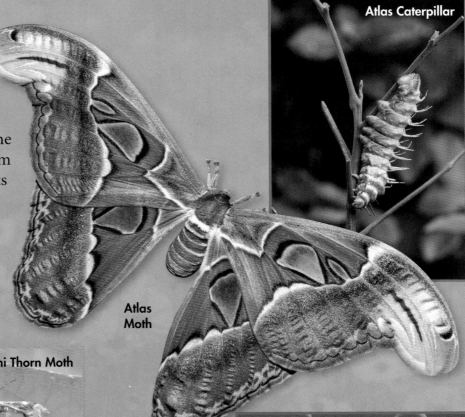

Atlas Caterpillar

Atlas Moth

Mini Thorn Moth

MINI THORN MOTH

This little guy is less than 1/10 inch (about 2 millimeters) across.

Io Moth Caterpillar

IO MOTH

The Io moth has a strange-looking caterpillar that has bunches of venomous spikes on its back. As an adult, the Io moth has two very prominent eyespots that make its hind wings look like an owl's face.

DID YOU KNOW?
The hawk moth is the world's fastest flying insect. It can travel at over 31 miles per hour (50 km/h).

Io Moth

23

CAMOUFLAGE AND MIMICRY

Camouflage and mimicry are similar. Both consist of shapes and colors that trick animals. Camouflage hides an insect by making it blend into its background, which makes it very difficult to see. If an insect has markings that break up its outline, it makes it even more difficult to find against its background surroundings. Insects and spiders are masters at camouflage because their exoskeletons can have all sorts of weird shapes and colors.

Mimicry is when an insect looks like something else. Sometimes the animal it mimics is more dangerous. A caterpillar that looks like a poisonous snake is likely to drive away predators. A tasty butterfly may mimic one that is full of toxins.

SNAKE CATERPILLAR

The vivid green snake caterpillar creates the look of a dangerous snake by pulling in its legs and expanding the end of its body, which has markings that look like snake's eyes. If it's threatened, it acts like it's going to bite!

Snake Caterpillar

Photocredit: Daniel Janzen

DID YOU KNOW?
Lichen spiders don't spin webs.

Sand Mottled Grasshopper

SAND MOTTLED GRASSHOPPER

Sand mottled grasshoppers blend in perfectly with the loose, sandy soil where they live. They forage on the ground, occasionally climbing up on stalks of grass.

This female velvet ant is actually a wingless wasp.

Lichen Spider

OLEANDER HAWK MOTH

The oleander hawk moth is also named the army green moth for the colorful green and white pattern on its wings that looks like army camouflage.

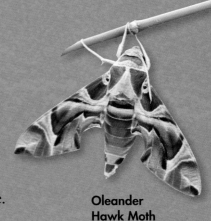
Oleander Hawk Moth

LICHEN SPIDER

Lichen spiders cling to tree trunks or branches that are covered with lichen. Their unique pattern and colors hides them perfectly as they wait to ambush their prey.

Leaf Mimicking Grasshopper

SCORPION FLY

The scorpion fly has a coiled tail that mimics the look of a scorpion. Its stinger isn't really a stinger at all.

Robber Fly

LEAF MIMICKING GRASSHOPPER

The leaf mimicking grasshopper mimics a dead leaf in the jungle.

Scorpion Fly

ROBBER FLY

This robber fly mimics a bumble bee.

WRAP-AROUND SPIDER

During the day, the wrap-around spider can wrap its body around a twig and make itself virtually invisible to predators. These spiders build webs at night, which they take down by the morning.

HUMMINGBIRD HAWK MOTH

The hummingbird hawk moth is frequently mistaken for a hummingbird as it flies from flower to flower. The wings of this moth make a loud humming sound just like the sound of a hummingbird's wings. Unlike most moths, it flies during the day and at night.

Hummingbird Hawk Moth

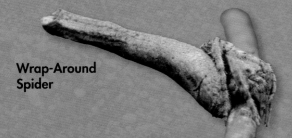
Wrap-Around Spider

IS IT AN ANT, A SPIDER, OR SOMETHING ELSE?

More than 300 different species of spiders are known to mimic the outward appearance of ants. Most ant-mimicking spiders have a "false waist" that is covered with reflective hairs to make them look as if they have the three-segmented bodies of ants. They position their two front legs so they look like an ant's antennae. In addition, they also adopt a zig-zag movement that is more like an ant than a spider.

Asian Ant Mantis

ASIAN ANT MANTIS

As a nymph, the Asian ant mantis mimics a black ant. When it becomes an adult, it loses its black-ant look.

Bird Dung Spider

DiD YOU KNOW?
Many predators dislike ants. By mimicking ants, spiders may avoid being eaten.

BIRD DUNG SPIDER

During the day, the bird dung spider sits on a leaf with its legs all tucked under itself. Birds and wasps think it's an unappetizing glob of bird droppings so they avoid it. These spiders also have another type of aggressive mimicry. They give out a scent that mimics the scent of a specific type of female moth. The male moths come and then the spiders capture them for food.

Bush Cricket nymph

Flickr Photocredit: gbohne

BUSH CRICKET

The bush cricket nymph mimics an ant to hide within an army of ants.

Kerengga
Ant-Like
Jumper

KERENGGA ANT-LIKE JUMPER

The Kerengga ant-like jumper is actually a jumping spider that mimics the Kerengga (or weaver ant) in the way it looks and acts. Two black patches on its jaws mimic the large compound eyes of the ant. The male's front legs look like a larger ant is carrying a smaller ant.

The Kerengga ant-like jumper splits its jaw from side-to-side to reveal its fangs.

The Kerengga ant-like jumping spider looks a whole lot like the real ant pictured here.

TOAD BUG

In its under-water home, the big-eyed toad bug looks just like the rocks it sits on.

Toad Bug

Scorpion Mimic Jumping Spider

Red Sword-Grass Moth

SCORPION SPIDER

The scorpion mimic jumping spider spreads its forelegs to mimic a scorpion.

RED SWORD-GRASS MOTH

The red sword-grass moth is cleverly disguised as a piece of broken twig.

CENTIPEDES, MILLIPEDES, & PILL BUGS

Centipedes, millipedes, and pill bugs are not actually insects, but they are also arthropods as insects are. Their preferred home is moist, decaying leaf litter in forests or around building foundations. Outdoors, they are very beneficial since they prey on other pest insects. They're not harmful to clothes, furniture, or other household items, but they can be somewhat scary-looking when seen indoors.

Centipedes and millipedes are closely related to insects. Pill bugs are sort of like a distant cousin. They're arthropods as well, but they're in a whole different category. They are more closely related to shrimp and crabs than to centipedes, millipedes, and insects in general.

Centipede

CENTIPEDES

Centipede means "one hundred legs," but, depending on the species, these arthropods can have as few as 15 pairs of legs or as many as 171 pairs. The legs on their first segment are not for walking. Instead, they are fangs that they use to inject venom into their prey. Centipedes always have a single pair of legs on each of their segments while millipedes have two pairs of legs on most body segments.

Centipede

DID YOU KNOW?
Centipedes can regenerate lost legs. Most centipedes run extremely fast.

Amazonian Giant Centipede

The Amazonian giant centipede can grow up to 12 inches (30.5 centimeters) long.

PILL BUGS

Pill bugs are land crustaceans related to shrimp, crabs, and lobsters. They're sometimes called doodle bugs or roly polies because of their ability to roll up into tight balls. Like their sea creature cousins, pill bugs breathe through gills. They need moist environments to breathe, but they can't survive in water.

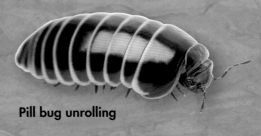

Pill bug unrolling

Sometimes male millipedes give female millipedes back rubs by walking on their backs with their hundreds of feet.

Flickr Photocredit: berniedup
Millipedes only have three pairs of legs when they hatch.

Millipede

MILLIPEDES

Millipedes don't actually have one thousand legs like their name suggests. The record for the number of legs is 750 making it the leggiest creature on Earth. Millipedes date back to prehistoric times when they grew to over 6 feet 7 inches (2 m) in length. Modern species sometimes reach lengths of 15 inches (38 cm).

CRICKETS, KATYDIDS, AND MORE

Grasshoppers, crickets, and katydids are all in the same family of insects. These insects look very similar to each other, but there are a few ways to tell them apart. Grasshoppers are generally larger than crickets and katydids. Even though they are larger, they have shorter antennae than crickets and katydids have. Grasshoppers are generally green or colors that blend in with their surroundings since they are active during the day. Crickets usually have a paler green, brown, or black color to hide in the shadows at night. Both crickets and katydids are active at night and "sing" by rubbing their forewings together. Grasshoppers "sing" too by rubbing their hind legs against their forewings. Most crickets can only jump, but to escape their predators, grasshoppers can jump and fly.

Painted grasshoppers are also called barber pole grasshoppers.

LEAF KATYDID

Many katydids are green in color and they mimic spring-green leaves. Some Leaf Katydids mimic brown, decaying leaves with holes and tears in them. There are even some that have both green and brown in their wings to mimic a leaf in partial decay.

Leaf mimic katydids

Dead-leaf Katydid

Pink Katydid

Pink katydids, native to Borneo, look like color-changing leaves.

30

Rainbow Milkweed Locust

Locusts are grasshoppers that are powerful flyers. The colors of the rainbow milkweed locust warn predators that it's toxic.

FIELD CRICKET

Field crickets shed their skin eight or more times before they reach adult size.

DRAGON HEAD KATYDID

The dragon head katydid has heavy spines along the sides of its thorax.

Giant Weta Cricket

Wiki Photocredit: Dinobass

GIANT WETA CRICKET

One of the biggest insects on Earth, a giant weta cricket can weigh more than a mouse.

Dragon Head Katydid

Flickr Photocredit: berniedup

This alien-looking, 3-inch long (7.62 cm) spiny devil katydid uses its spines to discourage predators.

31

DAMSELFLIES, DRAGONFLIES, & MORE

Dragonflies, dobsonflies, and damselflies have similar names but only two are closely related. There are four features you can use to tell a dragonfly apart from a damselfly: shape and size of eyes, body shape, wing shape, and wing position when at rest. Both the dragonfly and the damselfly have large eyes, but a dragonfly's eyes take up most of its head and wrap around from the side of its face to the front. The damselfly always has space between its eyes. Dragonflies have bulkier, thicker bodies than damselflies. Damselflies have bodies that look like thin twigs. Both types of insects have two sets of wings, but if you look closely at a dragonfly's wings you'll see that they are different shapes. Its hind wings are larger than its front wings.

A single dragonfly can eat hundreds of mosquitoes every day.

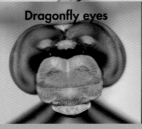
Dragonfly eyes

Damselfly eyes

DID YOU KNOW?
Dragonfly eyes touch while damselflies have space between their eyes.

DID YOU KNOW?
A human eye only has one lens, but each of a dragonfly's eyes has 30,000 lenses.

Damselfly

Dragonfly

DAMSELFLY
When a dragonfly rests, it keeps its wings opened flat like an airplane's wings. A damselfly folds its wings up and holds them together at the top of its back when it rests.

Hellgrammite

Dobsonfly

DOBSONFLY

Dobsonflies spend two to three years living underwater as larvae called hellgrammites. Strong jaws and two little hooks on their lower abdomens help them hold onto rocks to fight water currents. Eventually they crawl onto land, where they emerge as adult dobsonflies, living for about one week.

Close up of Dobsonfly

Larva of a dragonfly

Dragonfly larvae are hungry hunters. They will eat anything they can catch—including other dragonfly larvae!

Fossil of dragonfly

Wiki Photocredit: H. Zell

DID YOU KNOW?

Ancestors of dragonflies lived approximately 300 million years ago. They were huge with wingspans up to 25.6 inches (65 cm).

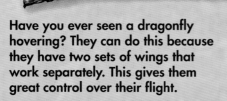

Have you ever seen a dragonfly hovering? They can do this because they have two sets of wings that work separately. This gives them great control over their flight.

ODD BUGS

Some insects live in societies and some live alone. Some make really loud sounds and some are quiet. Some can communicate with each other with chemicals and some use chemicals to make stinky smells to ward off predators. Some look like other animals or parts of plants so they can hide or ambush prey. Some are violent hunters and some are quiet and hide most of their lives. Some have amazingly beautiful colors and patterns like jewels and others are dull-colored like soil. Some are so odd-looking that, if they were larger, we would think they were aliens from another planet!

Walking Leaf Insect

WALKING LEAF INSECT

Walking leaf insects look so much like leaves that if they are sitting on a plant you might not even see them. They even have patterns that look like the veins in a leaf.

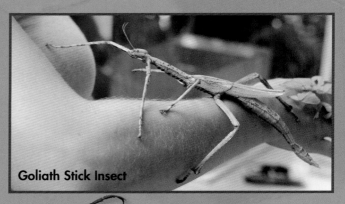

Goliath Stick Insect

The female Goliath stick insect can grow as long as 9.8 in (25 cm).

Malaysian Stick Insect

STICK INSECT

Stick insects are also known as walking sticks. They resemble the twigs where they live. Some get as long as 21 inches (51 cm) when their legs are outstretched.

Walking Stick Insect

34

GIANT PRICKLY STICK INSECT

The giant prickly stick insect looks more like a cactus than a twig.

Longhorn Beetle

Giant Prickly Stick Insect

LONGHORN BEETLE

Most longhorn beetles have antennae that are much longer than their bodies. Some even have what appear to be hairy tufts wrapped around their antennae.

LANTERNFLY

The lanternfly is a bug with decorative patterns. It grows a long and narrow snout, which acts as a straw to suck sap from trees and juice from flowers and fruit.

This lanternfly rests with its wings open.

Lanternfly

ALLIGATOR BUG

The alligator bug has a funny-looking, peanut-shaped head and a bulky body. Wrapped up inside its awkward shape is a secret weapon. When threatened, it opens its wings to reveal two fake eyes.

Alligator Bug

35

CHECK OUT THESE OUTRAGEOUS ODD BUGS!

Cicada

CICADA

Cicadas make buzzing and clicking sounds. The male cicadas use vibrating membranes on their abdomens to make the sounds. Some types of cicadas disappear for 13 or 17 years. Scientists believe these life cycles help the cicadas evade predators for the short time they are adults.

Spiny Fungus Beetle

SPINY FUNGUS BEETLE

Spiny fungus beetles are attracted to anything that smells musty.

DID YOU KNOW?
Some cicadas can make sounds that are almost 120 decibels. That's as loud as a chainsaw!

Planthopper

PLANTHOPPER

Some planthoppers have the strangest features of any insect. Wax-tailed planthoppers change the nutrients of the plant material they eat into long, strange-looking wax plumes.

DID YOU KNOW?
Planthoppers are fast and agile jumpers.

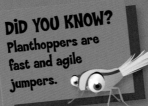

Wax-Tailed Planthopper

Flickr Photocredit: ggallice

GLOBE-TOPPED TREEHOPPER

The globe-topped treehopper looks something like a helicopter. The globes on its head aren't eyes or antennae. Some scientists believe that the weird head structures are designed to deter predators from eating them.

Globe-Topped Treehopper

Treehopper

Wasp Mantidfly

TREEHOPPER

Treehoppers are related to cicadas and leafhoppers. They have sharp pointed spines on their backs, which makes them look like thorns on plants. To eat, these bugs poke holes in tree branches and suck up the sugary sap. Each type of treehopper lives on a specific type of host plant.

WASP MANTIDFLY

With its folded-under arms, the wasp mantidfly looks a lot like a praying mantid on its front half. Its back half looks like a wasp body. But in reality, the wasp mantidfly is not related to either insect! It is in a family of insects called lacewings or net wings.

LEAFHOPPER

Leafhoppers are able to jump up, backwards, and sideways due to the design of their hind legs. They're also able to fly to avoid their predators.

Leafhopper

PEST BUGS

Insects are fascinating but they also bite us, sting us, suck our blood, infest our homes, attack our food, and sometimes carry deadly diseases.

CRANE FLY

Crane flies, nicknamed daddy longlegs, look like giant mosquitoes with very long legs.

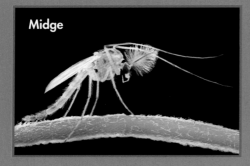

Midge

MIDGE AND GNAT

Midges and gnats are common names for a large number of small, annoying flies. They form swarms in the air, especially near standing water.

This close-up view shows a fly's face in all its hairy glory.

FLY

There are more than 120,000 species of flies in the world. Flies seem harmless enough, but they are known to carry diseases such as cholera and tuberculosis. Flies don't have any teeth. Instead, each fly has a long tongue called a proboscis. It uses its tongue like a straw to suck up food.

Gnat

THE LIFE CYCLE OF A FLY

Fly eggs

Fly larvae (maggots)

Empty fly pupal cases

Newly emerged fly

Each female fly lays approximately 500 eggs in her lifetime in batches of about 75. The eggs are white and they look like grains of rice. Within a day, the larvae, called maggots, hatch from the eggs. The maggots live and feed on organic material, such as garbage, dead animals, or poop. They enter a pupa stage before developing into adult flies.

MOSQUITOES

Mosquitoes are small midge-like flies that are bloodsuckers. The red bump and itching that people experience after a mosquito bites them is an allergic reaction to the mosquito's saliva. There are more than 3,000 species of mosquitoes, but only three carry diseases deadly to humans.

Mosquito

Madagascar Hissing Cockroaches

ROACHES

There are more than 4,000 species of cockroaches all over the world. Most species live in forests, under the ground, or in caves, fields, swamps, and grassland. Cockroaches have been on Earth as far back as 320 million years ago. They are hardy insects that eat virtually anything.

PRAYING MANTIDS

A praying mantid holds its front legs in a folded, upright position. It looks like it's praying, but don't be fooled because these insects are deadly predators. If a bee or a fly comes close, the mantid extends its arms and grabs its dinner at lightning speed. Sharp spines on its forelegs allow it to grasp its prey tightly as it eats. Some larger mantids eat frogs, lizards, and even small birds.

If you sneak up on a praying mantid in your garden, you might be scared when it turns its head completely around to look at you. Mantids are unique among insects in their ability to swivel their heads 180 degrees.

Mantids only have one ear, which is located on the underside of their bellies. This ear is designed to detect the echolocation sounds of hungry bats.

DiD YOU KNOW?
Praying mantids must shed their outer skeletons in order to grow. This is called molting. A mantid will molt 5 to 10 times before reaching its full size.

A dead leaf mantid's face (left) and full body (right)

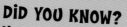

THE LIFE CYCLE OF A MANTID

Mantids produce foamy egg
sacs to hold their eggs.

The eggs take 3 to 6
weeks to hatch.

When they do hatch, up to
200 nymphs will emerge
from the sac.

Mantids are hard to see.
Some have bodies shaped
like leaves, parts of flowers,
or twigs, which help them to
camouflage themselves.
Their colors help them blend
into plants and flowers too!

**Giant Asian
Shield Mantis**

CHECK OUT THIS MASS AMOUNT OF MANTIDS

African Twig Mantid

When threatened, the spiny flower mantid raises its wings to make itself look like a larger creature with huge, golden eyes.

Spiny Flower Mantid

AFRICAN TWIG MANTID

Look closely! Is that a twig? No, it's an African twig mantid disguised as part of a plant.

Unicorn Mantid

Orchid Mantid

UNICORN MANTID

The unicorn mantid has two cones on its head that look like a horn.

Banded Flower Mantid

ORCHID MANTID

With its pink and white body, the orchid mantid hides inside an orchid to fool its prey.

Ghost Mantid

Wandering Violin Mantid

GHOST MANTID

The body of the ghost mantid looks just like a withered leaf. It is completely camouflaged in a pile of fallen leaves on the forest floor.

WANDERING VIOLIN MANTID

The body of the wandering violin mantid has all sorts of pieces that look like dried leaves. It bobs and weaves like a boxer before attacking its prey.

Devil's Flower Mantid

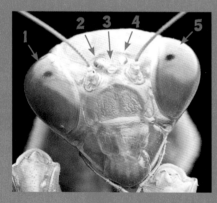
1 2 3 4 5

DID YOU KNOW?
Mantids have five eyes! Their two large compound eyes have hundreds of lenses to see images and colors. Mantids have three tiny simple eyes positioned in a triangular shape between their antennae.

FEATHER MANTIS

The feather mantis is also known as the giant Malaysian stick mantis.

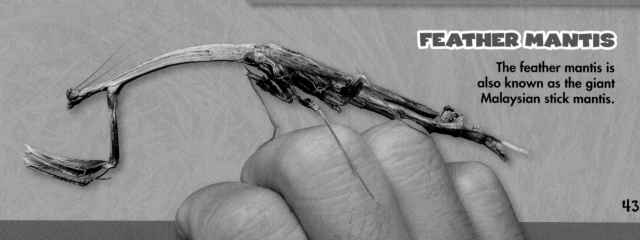

SPIDERS AND 8-LEGGERS

There are about 40,000 species of spiders and almost all of them are carnivorous, which means they eat insects and other animals to survive. Spiders aren't insects or true bugs. They are arachnids. All spiders have eight legs instead of the six legs that insects have. They also move differently than insects do.

Another major difference between insects and spiders is that most types of spiders spin webs to catch their prey. There are different types of spider webs: orbs, funnels, and sheets. No matter what type of web spiders weave, they do so with silk they produce themselves. The silk comes from spinneret glands on their abdomens and each gland makes a different type. Some of the silk is sticky, some is very fine, and some is for building different parts of the web. Spider silk is incredibly strong.

Long-Horned Orb-Weaver Spider

LYNX SPIDER

Lynx spider legs have many long, stiff, and sharp spines.

Green Lynx Spider

Wiki Photocredit: Chen-Pan Liao

CRAB SPIDER

Crab spiders look and move like crabs because they have longer front legs than back legs.

Crab Spider

SPINY ORB WEAVER

Spiny orb weavers have prominent spines on their abdomens. They look something like crabs.

Spiny Orb Weaver

LONG-HORNED ORB WEAVER

Just like other orb weaver spiders, long-horned orb Weavers build large circular webs. Scientists are not completely sure why this type of spider has such long horns but there's a good chance that the horns help deter potential predators.

Tarantula

TARANTULA

Even though they look very scary, tarantulas are quite docile. They rarely bite people and their bite is no worse than a bee sting. The largest tarantula by mass is the Goliath tarantula. It is large enough to capture and eat birds.

JUMPING SPIDER

Jumping spiders are the largest family of spiders, making up about 13% of all spider species. One unusually large pair of eyes stands out from their other simple eye pairs. When threatened or excited, they make very agile jumps.

Jumping Spider

Close-up of a jumping spider

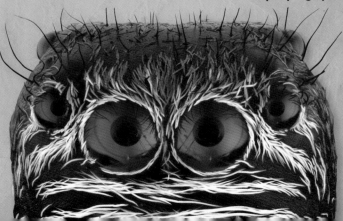

Wide-Jawed Jumping Spider

45

SPIDER WEBS

The trapdoor spider spreads trip lines made of web around its lair to detect prey.

Funnel web spiders wait for prey inside the funnel.

A trapdoor spider out of its burrow is a fearsome sight!

When a trip line is touched, the spider flips open its "door," leaps out, and grabs the unlucky meal.

Orb Weaver Spider

This spider is wrapping its prey in silk.

ORB WEAVER SPIDER

An orb weaver spider spins a zigzag mat to sit on. The mat is called a stabilimentum. Different types of orb weavers make stabilimentums in different shapes, but they all contain zigzags.

DiD YOU KNOW?
It takes a spider about an hour to build a web. Spiders usually build a new web every day.

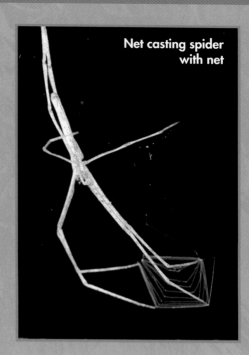

Net casting spider with net

NET CASTING SPIDERS

Net casting spiders have a unique way of catching prey. They fashion small webs that look like nets. They hold the nets in their front legs and stretch them out wide to catch passing prey.

DID YOU KNOW? Some spiders can jump up to 50 times their own length to grab prey.

Look at those eyes! Intimidating!

CHECK OUT THESE AMAZING ARACHNIDS

DADDY-LONGLEGS

Also called harvestmen, daddy-longlegs look like spiders, but they belong to a different species called Opiliones. Daddy-longlegs don't produce silk or make webs. They also don't have any venom.

WHIP SCORPION

Whip scorpions are arachnids that look similar to true scorpions. They don't possess a venomous sting like scorpions do. They give off an odor that smells like vinegar.

SCORPION

When food is scarce, scorpions can live on one insect per year.

Whip Scorpion

CHECK OUT THESE STRIKING SPIDERS

Black Widow

Brazilian Wandering Spider

BLACK WIDOW

The black widow is one of the world's most venomous spiders. It has a red marking shaped like an hourglass on its belly.

BRAZILIAN WANDERING SPIDER

Brazilian wandering spiders do not make webs. They move around at night, actively hunting their prey. They have powerful venom that they use to immobilize their meals.

Diving Bell Spider

The diving bell spider keeps an air bubble handy for breathing.

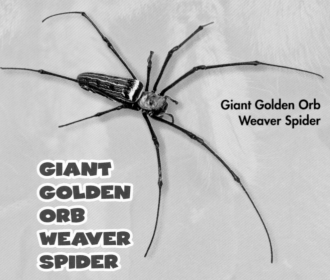
Giant Golden Orb Weaver Spider

DIVING BELL SPIDER

The diving bell spider is the only spider species that lives entirely underwater.

GIANT GOLDEN ORB WEAVER SPIDER

Female giant orb weaver spiders can be up to 8 inches (20 cm) across. They are one of the world's biggest spider species.

This giant spider drawing on the plains of Nazca, Peru, shows that people have been fascinated by these creatures since ancient times.

Ladybird Spider (male)

Ladybird Spider (female)

LADYBIRD SPIDER

The back half of the ladybird spider looks a lot like a ladybug. That's where this spider gets its name.

Mirror Spider

Wiki Photocredit: Doug Beckers

GIANT HUNTSMAN SPIDER

The giant huntsman spider can grow up to 12 inches (30 cm) wide. Its long legs can wrap around a human fist.

MIRROR SPIDER

Mirror spiders have shiny silver patches on their abdomens. They are small but sparkly!

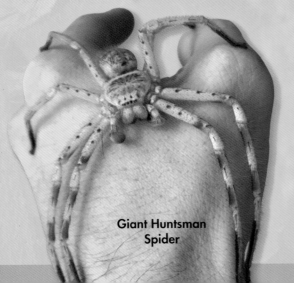
Giant Huntsman Spider

DID YOU KNOW?
Female wolf spiders carry their babies on their backs until they get big enough to strike out into the world.

TRUE BUGS

All bugs are insects, but not all insects are bugs. The major difference between true bugs and other insects is their mouthparts. True bugs use their mouthparts to suck juices, primarily from plants. They have a proboscis. It looks like a long beak and is used in the same way you use a straw to drink from a juice box. Other types of insects have a proboscis as well, but theirs are retractable, which means they can roll theirs up. The proboscis of a true bug can't be rolled back up. The other difference between true bugs and other types of insects is that they go through an "incomplete metamorphosis." Instead of going through the egg, larva, pupa, and adult stages, they hatch as nymphs, miniature versions of the adult bugs, right from their eggs.

Assassin Bug

LEAF-FOOTED BUG

In some species of leaf-footed bugs, the back legs are wide and may be leaf-like in shape. These bugs make a loud noise when they fly.

Leaf-Footed Bug

Lace Bug

Wiki Photocredit: shaners becker

LACE BUG

The unusual-looking lace bug has a lacelike pattern of ridges on its wings and upper body.

DID YOU KNOW?
The largest true bug in the world is the giant water bug.

ASSASSIN BUG

Assassin bugs use their strong beaks to stab their prey to death. They're often found on shrubs and garden plants as they search for prey. They're also called "kissing bugs" because they attack humans on the lips and give a painful bite.

Red and Black
Seed Bugs

Hibiscus Harlequin Bug
or Cotton Harlequin Bug

RED AND BLACK SEED BUGS

Red and black seed bugs are
sometimes called charcoal
seed bugs because they look
like dying embers from a fire.

Shield bugs, also
called stink bugs,
emit a smelly
chemical if you
disturb them.

The proboscis mouthpart on this
shield bug is covered with pollen.

WATER STRIDERS

Water striders can float, stand, skate, and walk
on water without getting wet. They have very
fine hairs on their feet that stay dry. These
hairs push against the water to create a tension
that holds them above the water surface.

AMBUSH BUG

As they blend
into their
surroundings,
ambush bugs wait
for their prey to come
near. Then, they quickly
grab the prey and poison it.

Ambush Bug

Water
Strider

51

WASPS AND HORNETS

Bees and wasps look similar, but there are some key differences. While bees are fuzzy, wasps have smooth, shiny bodies. Also, bees have plump bodies, but wasps are strongly segmented with very narrow waists.

Bees and wasps behave differently as well. Bees will usually leave people alone, but wasps are more aggressive. If they feel threatened, they will attack—sometimes as groups. Wasps carry powerful venom and they have smooth stingers that do not tear off their bodies, so they can sting many times in a row. Working together, a group of angry wasps can seriously hurt or even kill a human being.

Hornets are a type of wasp. They are large, up to 2.2 inches (5.5 cm) in length. Hornets are social insects that build big nests out of paper pulp that they create inside their bodies.

Cuckoo Wasp

ASIAN GIANT HORNET

Asian Giant Hornet

Some hornets are worse than others. The Asian giant hornet of Japan kills 30 to 40 people every year with its venomous sting.

Yellow Jackets

Wasps guard the entrance to their nests.

YELLOW JACKETS

Yellow jackets are among the most familiar wasps. Colonies can contain up to 100,000 adults!

Cuckoo Wasp

CUCKOO WASP

The cuckoo or emerald wasp has a metallic colored body.

52

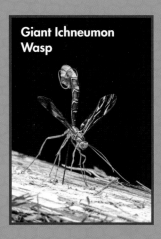
Giant Ichneumon Wasp

GIANT ICHNEUMON WASP

This wasp lays its eggs on grubs of other species. When the eggs hatch, the larvae eat the grub.

DID YOU KNOW?
Wasps make nests from paper. They chew up strips of bark and spit them out to form the building material.

Potter Wasp in flight

TARANTULA HAWK

One of the world's largest wasps is the tarantula hawk at nearly 1.5 inches (3.8 cm) long. This wasp kills tarantula spiders.

Potter Wasp nest

Tarantula Hawk

POTTER WASP

Potter wasps get their name from their mud nests, which look like little clay pots.

Wasp venom contains a chemical that makes other wasps get more aggressive. Don't swat a wasp near other wasps!

Wasp stinger

Wasp

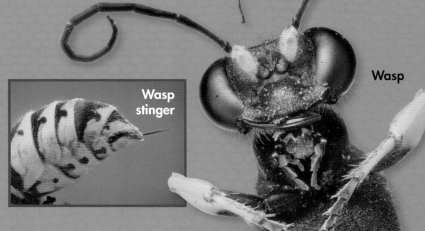

53

WEEVILS

Weevils are actually a type of beetle. There are more species in the weevil family than in any other beetle group. Weevils are usually dark in color and range from brown to gray to black. Some types have shiny hair or scales covering parts of their bodies. The most distinctive feature that most weevils have compared to other beetles is the shape of their heads. They have elongated heads that form snouts. Their mouths are at the end of their snouts. Some of them have snouts that are as long as their bodies!

Because weevils feed on plants both at the larva stage and as adults, they can be very destructive to crops. Some types infest stored grains and seeds and are often found in dry foods such as flour and cereal.

Acorn Weevil

LEAF-ROLLING WEEVIL

The leaf-rolling weevil makes its nest by rolling up leaves. This weevil begins by biting the leaf, which cuts it into shape. Then, the weevil folds the cut leaf in half, and rolls it up.

Leaf-rolling weevil nest

Flickr Photocredit: bob in swamp

Leaf-Rolling Weevil

Leaf-rolling weevil cutting leaf

ACORN WEEVILS

Acorn weevils pierce the soft tissue of young acorns, the seeds of oak trees, while the seeds are still growing. Their jaws are located at the end of their long snout.

DID YOU KNOW?
If you look at the polka dotted clown weevil under a microscope, it looks like it is covered in glitter.

PALM WEEVILS

The palm weevil prefers to feed on date palm trees but is a threat to palm trees all over the world.

Palm weevil adult

Palm Weevil larvae

Front view of a weevil

The polka dotted clown weevil has an exoskeleton that is covered in bright and shiny scales.

Giraffe Weevil

Gold Dust Weevils

GIRAFFE WEEVILS

The unusually long neck of the male giraffe weevil is used to fight other males. Giraffe weevils also use their necks to roll up leaves on their host plants to form nests.

GOLD DUST WEEVILS

Gold dust weevils get their name from their golden color. Here, male and female weevils hang out together on a leaf.

BUGS FEED THE WORLD

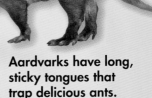

In this book, you have seen that insects do many interesting things. But one of the most important things bugs do isn't a behavior or an action; it's just being alive! Bugs are an essential food source for many animals, some of which eat nothing but insects. Without them, these animals would starve and the food chain would fall apart.

Aardvarks have long, sticky tongues that trap delicious ants.

A house wren brings a treat back to the nest to feed her chicks.

A chameleon eating a bug.

Fried scorpion-on-a-stick is a treat in some parts of the world.

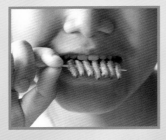

Crispy worm skewers are a great source of protein.

Humans don't depend on bugs to this extent, but people in many cultures do eat insects. Beetles are the most popular treat worldwide, followed closely by butterflies, ants, crickets, worms, and just about any other insect you can think of. These creatures are plentiful, full of protein, and tasty.

Are insects the sustainable future of the food industry? This view from a street vendor in Thailand suggests maybe they are!

Would YOU eat a bug? Give it a try! Animals everywhere depend on them; why not us? Bugs could feed the world… if we let them.